Love, Magic, & Coconut Oil

Copyright © 2020 by Arnetta "TABOO" Bullard
All rights reserved. No part of this book may be reproduced, scanned,
or distributed in any printed or electronic form without permission.
First Edition: February 2020
Printed in the United States of America
ISBN: 9781645508168

To God.
For the gift.
The passion.
& The purpose

A Seat At The Table ((of Contents))

Acknowledgement   x
Preface   xi

first comes LOVE...

Ashes   2

Ruins   3

To Her, With Love   5

SuperWoman   8

After Rupi Kaur   12

Ships and Anchors   14

Walls   15

No More   16

redruM   18

Cynical   20

Mourn   21

Stay Woke   24

Blue Skies   26

Invisible   29

Repentance   31

Mirror, Mirror   32

Then a dash of MAGIC...

Good Morning, Friend 34

The Days of Innocence 36

Screws & Bolts 40

Now 42

Nectar 44

Just A Friend 46

Wild Things Live Here 49

Thighs 50

Pinky Promise 52

Scarlet 54

Mermaid Confessions 57

Love Hard 59

Dwelling Place 62

And a little COCONUT OIL...

Lessons From My Dad... About God 65

Dejavu 68

No. You Cannot Touch My Hair. 71

Love, Magic, & Coconut Oil

After Nikki Giovanni — 74

Magic — 78

*"You are worthy
You are beautiful
You are deserving."*
Excerpt **"Mirror, Mirror"**

In No Particular Order...

I want to extend a heartfelt thank you to my grandmother, Lula Roberts, who has encouraged me since a young girl to pursue my dreams. She has been my saving grace even when I thought I was unworthy of being saved. She is everything a woman should be and everything I aspire to be. Plus, she thinks I am the best poet to ever grace this planet and so I thank her for her confidence in my gift.

I want to thank my friends for their continuous support at poetry nights near and far. #PrettyGang

I want to thank my sisters for Sister Chat, which keeps me motivated, keeps me laughing, and keeps me in check. My sisters and I talk every single day. They are my best friends. Thank God for our growth collectively.

I want to thank WillDaRealOne for allowing me to get on my very first mic at The Literary Cafe... on a comedy night. I was unfamiliar with the scene so I wasn't aware that it wasn't poetry night but he let me perform anyway. I am thankful for his kindness that night and his constant support and encouragement thereafter. Rest In Power, Will.

I want to thank IngridB and The BSide for being an extension of Will's kindness to me. She has shown me love since day one and I am beyond grateful and appreciative. I have been different versions of myself on TheBSide and she has accepted each layer of Taboo with open arms. Ingrid gave me my very first feature... and continues to support my gift fully. You are loved!

A special thank you to anyone who has ever watched me perform. Thank you for every 'REWIND!' and 'AMEN!'. Thank you for every encouraging word, hug, and social media follow after I left the mic.

Thank you to all of the Miami poets who have embraced me since the beginning... To every poet I have shared the stage with... To every poet I look up to... To every poet whose gift has inspired me.

Thank you all for supporting this work.
Thank you for allowing me to share my gift.

Preface

Love, Magic, & Coconut Oil is a body of work that encompasses my experiences as a woman, who has experienced her share of love, loss, healing, and rebirth. In its pages, readers are taken through a journey that exposes the core of who I am.

At age 12, I penned my very first poem; a guttural reaction to the shocking murder of a neighborhood friend, Dee. Since then, poetry has been a therapeutic way to sift through my feelings and share my journey on this emotional rollercoaster of life.

Although I have been writing and performing poetry for several years, this is my very first poetry book in publication. I have grown tremendously as a writer, and as a woman, since the start of my poetic career and I am proud to share this culmination of poetry with you.

I decided upon the title "Love, Magic, & Coconut Oil" after reviewing the nearly 60 poems that I wanted to compile for publication. Ultimately, I decided to condense this selection to thirty-four poems in honor of my 34th birthday this year (chosen as the release date for this work).

Each section features raw emotion based on personal experiences and provides an authentic view into my mind.

LOVE- Trust me, it is not what you think. This section explores the suffering and heartache of love. For a long time, I was unhappy and believed I needed to suck it up for the sake of maintaining a relationship that was the definition of unhealthy and toxic... for the sake of my kids, my pride, and simply for the sake of just being "in love". I put on a brave face for years until, ultimately, I learned to love myself first and foremost.

Then... the magic happened.

MAGIC- Last year, was the beginning of how I want to live the rest of my life! This section explores my experience beyond the mere idea of love and dives into my voyage of freedom. I have had the pleasure of realizing that how I want to be treated isn't an anomaly. These poems cover my journey of friendships, being desired, living on the wild side, and establishing genuine connections.

COCONUT OIL- This section is about my experience as a black woman, a black mother, a black HUMAN being. It is no easy feat living in this skin, but I am proud of it. Everyday.

It is my hope that you are able to see yourself along the pages of this book, recognize that your pain and your experiences are not exclusively your cross to bear, and ultimately know that life begins the moment you accept yourself- flaws and all, and LOVE YOURSELF unconditionally!

Thank you for reading.

I hope you enjoy!

LOVE

"Our love has become a galaxy
We cannot travel to
Without dying en route"
~excerpt **"Walls"**

Ashes.

Oh, how I loved him
Enough to set fire to myself
To keep him warm
Didn't know he'd love the smell
Of rotting flesh
Didn't think twice about turning to ash
Didn't expect him to like the feel
Of soot
Under his feet
Couldn't predict he'd morph into fire-eating dragon
And feed off of my pain
Only wanted to keep him warm
To love him whole
To light a path for him to walk into all of the potential I knew he possessed
Only lit the match because I hoped he would match my passion
Love me completely
With his whole self
But he was too broken
And I realized only after
It all went up in flames

Ruins.

As I watch him sleep
I wonder what he's going to do when I leave
I think about whether my exit
Will be the push
He needs
to reach his full potential
Or a shove
Off of the deep end
I hate that I still care
Either way
Hate that he is sleeping peacefully
And I am up watching the sun rise
With the rise and fall of his chest
Wishing he was this calm
In his waking moments
Wishing he was not storm
Wrecking our home
Without warning
Defacing the love we cultivated with bare hands
For over a decade
Wishing disaster wasn't his middle name
His heartbeat a constant call of war
When all I want to do is wave the white flag
And call a truce
Because I am tired of fighting
This man

TABOO

Ready to lay down my arms
And lay in his
for the last time
Heart heavy
A million pieces
To serve as a constant reminder
Of this moment
A true depiction of our union
He brought war to our doorstep constantly
And somehow always found peace
in the rubble
left behind

To Her, With Love.

Baby Girl, I pray you do better
I pray the man you find understands what he has found
in you
Able to truly respect your physical
and smart enough to understand
your mind is most beautiful
I pray love truly loves you
'Cause Lord knows mama's life has sung a Jazmine Sullivan tune

'Why do we love love
When love seems to hate us'

And hate me it did

I pray you NEVER go through all I've had to experience
The hurt and the pain
The regret
and the shame
I pray the man you fall in love with
loves you the same
Because anything less isn't worthy
I pray he spoils you
Pray he buys you nice things
Not because you are a gold digger
but because he recognizes a queen
I pray he cherishes you from head to navel ring

TABOO

from waist to toes and every inch in between
I pray you do better
I pray the man you love respects you
By YOUR definition of the word
Pray he listens to your concerns
and doesn't label them absurd
I pray he trusts you
enough to share his soul with you
If you mess up
I pray that he forgives you
I pray he kisses you just because
Pray he adores the woman you are
Pray he realizes he doesn't deserve you
I pray he thanks his lucky stars
Baby Girl, I pray you do better
I pray you don't marry young
Pray you get the chance to live your life
before becoming somebody's mother
before becoming some man's wife
But if you take that path
I pray that it is meant to be
I pray it doesn't bring you the same pain
that it has brought me
I pray he means the vows he speaks on your wedding day
Sickness and in health
For richer or poorer
Forsaking all others
Until death do you part
No matter what trials you face

I pray your love remains strong
I pray it stands the test of time
You are special, Baby Girl
You deserve better than a love like mine.

SuperWoman.

My grandmother is SuperWoman
Fully equipped with the power to do any and every thing for any and every one who asks for or needs her help
She is powerful
Powered by the spirit of God which resides in her
Very rarely have I heard my grandmother say 'no'
And mean it
And in all honesty I cannot recall her saying no at all
Raising three little girls who weren't necessarily her responsibility at all
My grandmother adorned herself in an invisible cape and set out to conquer the world daily
And we watched her conquer it all daily
We sat with bated breath intrigued by the magic concealed within her small stature
She showed us
Women are powerful
And limitless
We watched her day in and day out be the fixer of every problem
The answer to every prayer
We absorbed her innate ability to be mother, cook, and maid
Lover of God, wife, cousin, niece, employee, and everything in between
Needless to say, my grandfather was a lucky man
These days we each sit bewildered by the men lucky enough to have direct descendants of SuperWoman standing by their sides
We question our decisions to fall in love
Head first

And without reason
With men inherently incapable of appreciation of our bloodline
But that type of love is all too familiar to us
See, I told you my grandfather was a lucky man
Paralyzed from the waist down
He grew accustomed to having my grandmother do everything for him
And she grew accustomed to bending over backwards but never breaking under the pressure customarily acquired when carrying the weight of the world on your shoulders
She never broke a sweat because she loved him
And being SuperWoman was her way of showing him the full scope of her love
Like eagle wings stretched far and wide
The span of her love was immeasurable
And we watched
Subconsciously preparing ourselves to walk in grandma's shoes
We grew up and fell in love with men who were paralyzed
But not because of botched robbery attempts at the hands of gun wielding gangstas
Our men weren't lucky enough to be physically impaired
They are the worst kind
Crippled by the hands they were dealt on this side of the horizon
We fell in love with the mama's boys and the emotionally abused
Men so far detached from reality they don't realize their distinctive and abundant shortcomings
We fell in love with the angry men with spirits wounded from hardships completely incomparable to the struggles we faced as little girls
Men whose mamas ain't ever done an ounce of coke and whose fathers never beat them like he had a point to prove to God

TABOO

Men whose parents didn't throw them away
But see they weren't descendants of SuperWoman
They weren't raised to use their issues as fuel to propel them into the greatness God promised they would achieve
Their blood is tainted by weaknesses they are too manly to admit
And brazen egos that have been known to destroy many a coward
I mean, many a man
I mean, define MAN
We have yet to swallow the large horse pills lodged in each of our throats begging us to accept that they don't fit that definition
And we refuse to swallow or acknowledge its existence
Because our grandmother is SuperWoman
And she has taught us that the power of a woman is limitless
And so we strap on our invisible capes and remain loyal to the men we love who have yet to acknowledge our bloodline
Men like my grandfather
Lucky until the day he died
To have SuperWoman standing stoically at his side
Unwavering
We believe in our power to change them
So we never stop praying for them
We see the men God created them to be from clay when we were taken from their ribs
We see Adam in them so we fall in line to be helpmeet
Helping them meet the challenges carved into their roots by fate
And we are faithfully
Mothers to their children
We are friends
Lovers

And wives
We are strong shoulders for them to cry on
We are breadwinners without complaint
We are constant forgivers of their betrayal
We are prayer warriors for their souls
We are cooks and maids
We are unconditional lovers of their potential
And we know that one day they will see our grandmother in us
And on that day these men
Our paralyzed men whom we love deeply and without reason
Will come to love, honor, cherish
and respect
The direct descendants of SuperWoman
They are so lucky to have

TABOO

After Rupi Kaur.

"Tell them I was the warmest place you knew and you turned me cold"

Tell them how many times I forgave you before the apologies even left your lips
Tell them how often apologies never came
Tell them how you hurt me
How my pain has morphed into anger
Tell them how many times I have begged you
Pleaded for you to finally be a man
Tell them how you failed me
Tell them how you continue to fail me
How you walk around like things are sweet when they are rotten to the core
Tell them how rotten you are on the inside
How you can't seem to manage being anything more than THAT
Tell them how much I loved you
How I tried to love you into something better
Tell them how it was never reciprocated
Tell them how your mother and father never taught you how to love the right way
Tell them how you have no idea what love really is
How you imagine it is this thing we are so caught up in
Tell them you're unsure
Tell them I said you're too fucking old to be unsure
Tell them it will be too late for you to figure it out soon
Tell them I am tired of waiting

Tell them I have waited for far too long for the impossible to take place
Tell them I can no longer be the warm place for you to rest
Tell them I am drained
Tell them my heart needs time to heal
Tell them forgiveness has an expiration date
Tell them your time is up

And when they ask
if you believe
there can be redemption on the other side of this pain
Tell them
I was the warmest place you knew
and you turned me cold

<u>Ships and Anchors.</u>

Love anchors the soul
Keeps you grounded
when the world seems to be flipped upside down
Keeps you standing
when life deals a blow that weakens your knees
Makes sure you are supported
Provides the strength you need to make it through just one more day
Love
Is supposed to be an anchor
And sometimes it is just that
A weight
Rusted
And noisy
Tied around your heart
Dragging you to the bottom of an ocean you regret setting sail on
Love
Is supposed to bring you peace
But there is nothing peaceful about drowning

Walls.

The history between us
Has become a border
Separating our hearts
Patrolled by guards with loaded rifles
Ready to shoot
If either of us crosses the line
And so
We have learned to keep our distance
Close enough to hurt but never close enough
to love
completely
I often wonder if you'll ever be brave enough to scale the wall
To cross over into once chartered territory
To go the extra mile
And right all of the wrongs that I have lost count of
But I know better
I know it just isn't in you to love deeply
And so
I choose to stay on my side
Growing more and more distant daily

Our love has become a galaxy
We cannot travel to
Without dying en route
And for once
I choose to live

No More.

I can literally feel my heart breaking
Every day I wake up
And try to make you a distant memory
But our son
Has your eyes
And I realize
There are parts of you
I will never be able
To wash away
Though I tried
In scalding hot showers
To remove fingerprints
From my body
You molded me
Broken
Pierced my heart with
Words
That you can never unsay
And I cannot
Unhear
No matter how many margaritas I drink
To ease the pain
Some things
Are unforgettable
Shattered hearts remain
Unfixable

Never fully whole again
You have done it this time
Made a believer out of me
For all the years I doubted
That you were poison
For all the years I ingested
Without fear
Today I accept the demise
Of what we created
Today
I breathe new life
Today I let dead things lie
Place flowers atop headstone
And I walk away
from it all

redruM.

On the day he threatens to murder you
With rage in his eyes
venom on his tongue
And intention in his hands
That keep coming too close to your face
Your voice will quiver
But you will still shout back at him
Refusing to cower under the weight of his words
Although you know that broken men are the most dangerous

On the day he threatens to murder you
With your kids mere feet away
You will replay possible outcomes in your mind
As he spews his hatred loud enough for the neighbors to become concerned
Your heartbeat will quicken
But you will still shout back at him
Refusing to let him see you sweat
Although you know that words have power
And powerless men are the most dangerous

On the day he threatens to murder you
You will sleep with one eye open
And a knife next to your bed
With your children in the next room
In case he decides to finally be a man of his word

When morning comes
You will pack all of your things
And leave him
For good
Without so much as goodbye
Because you know goodbyes are triggering
For men who've lost control
And men without control are the most dangerous

On the day he threatens to murder you
You will realize just how toxic your love has become
Your heart will shatter
You will cry deeply
And feel pain even deeper than that
But you will survive
Because you will not stay around
After the day he threatens to murder you

TABOO

Cynical.

One day
I will believe in fairytales again
But today
I am too jaded
To believe in love

Mourn.

A part of me wants to cry
To mourn the death of our love
properly
Walk through New Orleans with a jazz band
Playing the blues for us
Sit shiva for seven days
While concealing my tears behind this black veil
And finally lay it all to rest
Ashes to ashes
Dust to dust
To watch it slowly descend out of reach
Giving it back to the earth
Throwing dirt on our memories
The way you often threw dirt on my name
Covering up all that used to be good
And pure
Saying a final farewell
To what I imagined would last forever
But life is funny that way I guess
Or love is
Either way the humor isn't lost on me
And so I am smiling
Through my tears
Because I know what once was
And this isn't it
Isn't even worthy to be called its remains

TABOO

I guess the vultures are well fed now
Can't even recognize whatever this once was
And so I'll take your word for it
And say that this was love
This was everything when nothing else mattered
This was intoxicating before the legal age to consume alcohol
This was follow me to college because we couldn't commit to goodbye
This was family when family turned its back on me
This was shoulder to cry on when your grandmother died
This was hand to hold when both of my grand dads passed away
This was comforting back rub when my stepdad got his wings
This was puppy love that aged like fine wine at first
But grew to smell like rotten cheese instead
This was a series of unfortunate events that could have been avoided
had you known what love was in the first place
This was life lessons on forgiveness I never signed up for
This was every life lesson I didn't know I needed up until now
Like learning how to walk away when it becomes toxic
Like now
Like learning how to say goodbye
even when your heart tries to convince you
it can be repaired by the same hands that shattered it
Like now
Like learning to recognize a dead thing
And grieve it accordingly
Like now
Like knowing when enough is enough
And nailing the coffin shut
As tears stream down your face

And the final goodbye escapes your lips
So...
Goodbye
now, my love

Stay Woke.

Depression beckons me to sleep
For as long as I'd like
Whispers softly for me to take forever if I have to
And so I listen
Lay my head on down pillow
Close my eyes to slumber
With plans to sleep this life away
But then anxiety calls
Yells loudly from the other room
With voices that sound so much like my children
Keeps me awake
Long enough to feel that my heart is still beating
Forcefully
I imagine it can be seen through my blouse
I imagine everyone notices that its rhythm isn't normal
That there shouldn't be this much noise in my chest
And after all of this pain
I don't understand how I haven't flatlined yet
With orders not to resuscitate
Because some things just aren't worth fighting for
Aren't worth waving the white flag
Because though I do not fight
I also do not surrender
Or settle
I just want to walk away before the dust settles

I often imagine I am anywhere but here
Though I smile
And laugh
And pick up the broken pieces
As they fall in my wake
I've been walking in circles trying to maintain this facade
Sleep walking
Never at rest
Even when the eternal tempts me with its sweet solitude
Even when depression beckons me to slumber parties parts of me don't want to resist
The voice of anxiety is eerily familiar
And it always serves as a constant reminder to
stay woke

Blue Skies.

I know we've all seen the commercials
Who does depression hurt: everyone
Well, I'm here to confess
that just isn't true
Depression
only hurts the depressed
Just like this recession
only hurts those whose jobs and finances are on recess
And I know because both of these things apply
Tonight you may see me with a smile on my face
but truth is
I'm broken inside
When I am alone in my room
without provocation I cry
And it only hurts
me
'Cause this broken part of me
nobody ever sees
Not even my kids
And for them I've learned to hold it all in
Because they know Mommy is strong
And I know
They've got it all wrong
But I refuse to be the one to tell them
To share my sadness and pain
So I put up this facade always

Holding on to my tears until
they fall asleep
Refusing to allow even a single tear to leak
'Cause the worst part about living with grief
is having your daughter look you in the eye
and ask
Mommy, what's wrong
The worst part is having your 3-year-old pat your back
reassuring you it's gonna be OK
Leading her on to believe Mommy is just having a bad day
When truth is
Mommy has been having bad days ever since she knew what days were
And I'd love to explain that to her
But I'm miserable
And I don't want company
So I smile
At her and anyone else around
And would you believe the world never stops
its rotation
I think of the documentary
The Bridge
and how brave the suicidal must be
To stand on that rail
with waves crashing beneath
they just leap
I think of how broken and depressed they must be
And I weep incessantly
Because these people remind me
of me

TABOO

But I am not brave enough
so there will never be footage of my leap
Though I hold fast to my belief
that even if the world could see what I see
my depression would still only hurt
Me

Invisible.

Do you see me?
Really see me?
Through this smile that I've perfected
To cover all of the imperfections?
Do you see me?
Do I look happy to you?
Do you care enough to recognize if I am truly happy
With you?
Do you notice if my smile ever reaches my eyes
Or if it stops at the creasing of my cheeks?
Do you notice the broken parts of me at all?
The jagged edges that keep my tongue sharp
Like two-edged sword?
Do you see me?
Really see me?

I just want someone to see me
To trace their fingers along all of the broken pieces
And avoid being cut by them
To cut through the caution tape around my heart
And find genuine love hidden there
To cherish the imperfections of my body
And explore every inch of my skin with pleasure
To understand the weight I've had to carry ever since I could form memories
And consciously decide not to be just another burden to me

TABOO

I want someone to recognize the reasons I have been angry
And acknowledge that I have had every reason to be angry
To know and appreciate that I have lived in pain
And decide to never be the reason behind my pain
To recognize that I come with baggage
And choose to help me carry the load
I want someone to love me
Wholly
To see me
Completely
To know perfection does not exist in these bones
But I want them to understand these bones are all that I have
These dead bones
Yearning to be revived

Do you see me?
Standing here?
Waiting for you
To love me
Without apology
Or reservation?
Because I am here
Trying my hardest not to be invisible
anymore

Repentance.

I want to ask forgiveness
For the times I made a god out of him
Worshipped at his feet
Made our bed a holy communion
For the times I allowed him to
Take
and eat
though he be undeserving
always

Forgive me, Father
For I have sinned.

Mirror, Mirror.

You deserve love
the steadfast kind
Persistent
on days you'd prefer to give up
Tireless
on days you are exhausted
from being everything to everyone
but yourself
You deserve happiness
that shakes you from the inside
Out
You are worthy
You are beautiful
You are deserving.

I love you.
Always
and foremost.

MAGIC

"Your smile is a welcome mat at the front door
Letting me know it is okay
To walk inside"
~excerpt *"Dwelling place"*

Good Morning, Friend.

Last night
you kissed me
And for a second
I imagined we were more
than just friends
Closed my eyes
To relish the moment
And opened them to find yours
Resting on my face
A smirk dancing across your lips
I smiled
And looked away
Never able to meet your gaze
Afraid you will see into my soul
And know all of this want
That exists inside of me
For you
And then you kissed me again
like you sensed this fire
burning inside
But your mouth
Never an extinguisher
Only fans the flames
Stroked my face
In between moments of exhale
To let me know that it's ok to trust you

To let go
Of inhibitions
And let down walls
I am always mindful to keep up
Around you
You let me know the feeling is mutual
You like me
too
Possibility lingers on your tongue
A delicacy I cannot yet afford to indulge in
Completely
You, my friend, are
The sweetest taboo
And yet
Only a friend
still

The Days of Innocence.

I remember when being in love was easy

When the biggest argument we had was whether or not he'd walk me home
from school or choose to hurry home to go ride his bicycle that day

And I know many people say this but I remember those notes asking me to go steady
And all those times I checked no only to regret my decision the next day
once I saw him holding hands with another girl
Not as cute
Not as smart
Some second rate version of me

I remember all I had to do was speak to him in the cafeteria and offer him my corn
on Pizza Fridays and he'd dump her as if I had checked yes the first time around

Those were the days...

The days when infidelity didn't exist because boys knew when
they had the best girl in the school on their arm and they wouldn't dare risk it
When boys made you cry because they liked you and not because they were

mere inconsiderate selfish imbeciles with hidden agendas

When little girls sneaked and kissed little boys behind the portables
during PE and then afterwards avoided looking in their faces

When little boys asked little girls to let them 'rip' knowing deep down they
wouldn't get to see any of the other bases
after one

See, I remember the days of innocence

Playing soccer in my grandmother's yard
trying hard to deter the gaze of that nosey neighbor
who thought all little girls were fast
Even those dressed like little boys
Me
Jumping fences and playing football in the street
Me

Too shy to even kiss my boyfriend on the cheek
and not run away
See, I ran every day
Every single time he chose to walk me home instead of riding his bicycle
When the fights were avoided and he bought me ice cream and lollipops
from the corner store we always passed on our way home
Walking hand in hand
Quickly breaking physical contact whenever a car rode by

Those innocent moments of having innocent love

TABOO

Limitless love
Love that we'd swear could reach the moon and back but we never really knew
what that meant
Untested
Unwavering
Love

'Check yes or no and if you check no I'll forgive you tomorrow when you see me
with her' type of love

Boy...
Those were the days

When arguments ended with your mom calling me to ask what's going on because her little boy is walking around the house like he's lost his best friend
See, she knew we were best friends
And this boyfriend girlfriend mess was just our way of being closer
As if we needed an excuse for that
You lived a block away
if that
We were together every day
in school and out
Elementary soul mates
Bonding over school uniforms and playground antics
We expressed our love by hanging upside down together on the monkey bars

I remember we kissed there once
on the cheek of course

You drew our names in the dirt with a stick
and then we played sword fight

I won

And I'm pretty sure you let me but I took the win nonetheless
Because back when love was easy you weren't full of pride
And you didn't mind losing some stupid little boy game that your girlfriend
shouldn't have been playing anyway

You were just like every other little boy in love

Sometimes you made me cry
but most of the time
Most of the time you walked me home from school
and those were the days I remember most

Screws & Bolts.

I used to love a boy that couldn't read
Even though he became the author of many obituaries
He couldn't write me a love note to save his life
Though I wanted so desperately to save his life
I think of boys like him
Too many to name
Who are handed guns before books
Who are taught the business of the streets
Before anyone tells them they have no business in these streets
I think of how unfair life is that way
How their mothers love them into damnation
Groom them into walking headlines
and breaking news stories
I remember my heart breaking
Every time I would watch the news stories
Not knowing if his murder would be televised that day
Wondering what his obituary would say
But never wanting to read his truth that way
I remember trying to teach him to read
The embarrassment he tried to conceal
As he concealed a gun in his waistband
I remember wanting to save him
Thinking his life would not be wasted if I could only get him to read
I remember how foreign words seemed on his tongue
And regret not speaking his language

Wanted to tell him he was loved
But was too afraid the message would get lost in translation
We were from the same place
But lived two different realities
He was the embodiment of preschool to prison pipeline
Before the term was ever coined
And I
With my ambition and the world at my fingertips
Only wish I could have saved him
But my love just wasn't enough
To reroute his destiny
Especially since he believed
The streets loved him better
Than I ever could

TABOO

NOW.

I used to love you
But I couldn't admit it then
Couldn't wrap my mind around the boundaries we crossed
Tried keeping my heart out of it
But even my mind screamed to let you love me
And I believe you did
I knew it in my spirit
Without the words ever leaving your lips
It was in the way you looked at me
Hidden in plain sight
Behind your smile
I felt it even in the slightest touch from you
Electricity coursing through our bodies
Escaping from our fingertips
Feeding off of one another's energy
Everyone could see the love between us
Though we dare not speak its name

You used to love me
And it was easy
And it was pure
And it was everything I needed
And could not have
And cannot have
Yet still am very much in need of

I know its been a while but tell me
Do you still love me
Now

Nectar.

I closed my eyes and tasted the nectar
Dripping from your lips
Imagined your tongue in the spaces between
All the incomplete parts of me
Smiling at the memory
Or was it a premonition
Of things to come
See, I love when you come
Near me
Invading personal spaces I dare not keep you out of
You are beauty and beast
Packaged nicely
Your body is home to the type of animal
I've always wanted to be
The unruly kind
That lives on the edge and loves hard
Hardly admitting it along the way
I am fond of the situations we find ourselves in
Bodies touching
Ever so gently at times
But always rough when necessary
Always so very necessary
See I want to love the hell out of you
See your devils and raise you a few of my own
Don't know if you believe it is possible
But I'd be a fool to not give it a try

You make me think of mushy things
How sometimes love isn't found in the familiar places you expect it to be
Sometimes it is hidden
In the crevices
No one is supposed to look in to
Forbidden spaces
With "do not touch" signs hanging on the wall
Museums for the fragile
And the broken
Hearts pieced together with duct tape
Affixed to the walls
Waiting to be seen
And admired
And made whole

You make me think of love
When I should only be focused on forbidden fruit
And how sweet its nectar tastes
On my tongue

Just A Friend.

[In the tune of Biz Markie]
Oh baby you
You got what I need
But you say he's just a friend
You say he's just a friend

Just friends huh
Tell that to these butterflies in my stomach
That won't die down
Tell that to this quickened heartbeat
Beating out of my chest
Everytime you come around
Matter of fact, tell that to your lips
That always curve upward when you see me
That smile isn't a just friend kinda smile
It gives you away every time
Tell that to your arms
That always hold me a little too long
And always so close
Tell that to your hands
That fit perfectly interlocked with mine
Tell that to my body
That always finds its way into your bed
Tell that to these thoughts in my head
That are always wondering what you're doing
Whenever you aren't doing whatever this is with me

Mr. Single Single
Except on the days we link up
Those days we play doubles
We kiss like there is honey hidden inside of our mouths
And our tongues play like bees
Trying to harvest it
I love swapping spit with you
Friend
I love the way you shift the energy of the room
Friend
I love watching Netflix with you until we fall asleep
Friend
I love play fighting with you
Friend
Because you get all fake mad
And I get to pretend I am sorry
Though I am not
I guess I just love "making up" with you, Friend
I love sleepovers and waking up to you, Friend
I love when I open my eyes and catch you watching me
Friend
I love watching you
Breathe,
Friend
Your breath reminds me that I am still alive
And don't we all need gentle fine ass reminders sometimes
I love making vague plans with you
Friend

TABOO

Like someday we're gonna go some place just for the sake of saying we went together
But we don't go together
Friend
I mean, we fit
Boy, do you fit
but at the end of the day we're just friends
Friend
That's why these butterflies confuse me
This heartbeat of mine is confusing
And I know you feel it too because you've shared there's something under the surface brewing
Maybe one day we'd both be willing to stop and smell the roses
That have been blooming
Right under our noses
for years

In the meantime though

I'll say he's just a friend
I'll say he's just a friend
Oh baby you!

Wild Things Live Here.

Good women can be wild too
And that is the best part of us
Isn't it
Those moments of wild
Freedom
Reckless abandon
We want our hair pulled
To be taken roughly
Throats grabbed intensely
And kissed with wild passion
From men capable of soaking sheets
With our juices
Messy eaters
That get a kick out of how good
we taste and feel
from the inside
We are starved
So hungry for men who can stare directly into the sun
Without leaving damage in their wake
For beasts who hold both sun and moon in their hands
We want to be conquered
By those who make us comfortable enough to be wild
But recognize the good within us
Because it is so good
To be acknowledged
wholly

Thighs.

He said he loves my thighs
And I love everything they wrap around
Like his body
Back sculpted
Marble turned flesh
He is beautiful
Every inch of him
And I'm still counting them one by one
Even his hands
An extension of his manliness
Perfectly sized to grip these thighs
This ass
These curls atop this head
When we kiss
He reminds me that I ain't as hard as I pretend to be
But I keep on pretending anyway
Afraid to let my guard down
Though he be man enough to catch me
Though he be strong enough to lift me
Squat my bodyweight at the gym
I be light work for him
I put in slight work for him
Though I don't always like that they touch
These thighs be ready to split at his command
Rough voice leaving throat
Enter my ear as growl

These thighs turn him animal
Beast
And I be proudly prey
Praying he chooses to stay
Between them
Kisses them in appreciation
Worships every dent and curve
This man said he loves my thighs
And I just love the way that he shows it

Pinky Promise.

He said he doesn't plan to go anywhere this lifetime
I wonder if I can get that written in blood
Or at the very least
If our pinkies could wrap around each other as confirmation
That he means what he says
I imagine he's a man of his word
An honest man
With good intentions
But the road to hell is paved with those
I feel I'm on the edge of a cliff
Ready to take that leap
If only to see if he is the truth
If he is willing to catch me
Even though the act itself seems
Impossible
I wonder
If he'd let me know
How he really feels
If it is only sexual for him
Because he remembers everything we did
I wonder if he remembers every single thing we did
Like staying up until sunrise
Talking for hours
I question if he understands how much of an aphrodisiac
Mental stimulation is
For me

I wonder if he'd share his darkest secrets
If he'd let me into places other women have never been given access to
If any of those places even exist
I wonder
If he'd be gentle
Even if I didn't come to him broken
If he'd fall in love with me
If my heart weren't off limits
And if he'd ever promise not to hurt me
I wonder if I could get that written in blood
Or at the very least
If our pinkies could wrap around each other as confirmation
The way our bodies once did

Scarlet.

Sometimes scarlet letters aren't stitched into our garments
But are instead worn like blood stains on our conscience
Reminding us that we have walked a mile in the shoes
Of the monsters we said we would never be
No one knows the extent of our relationship with the devil
Or how we've grown comfortable flirting with disaster he so willingly offers
He takes all of the bad things and makes them feel...
So good
Even though we know our dealings with him are no good
We have learned to embrace our secret sins
Because we are aware that no one can identify them from the outside looking in
We are no Hester Prynne
But there is more to us than what meets the naked eye
When we are exposed in our nakedness
There is no scarlet stitching to identify our lies
And we dare not confess or bare our souls at societal altars which offer only condemnation
No one will understand or willingly offer forgiveness if we speak our indiscretions aloud
So we keep them tucked away in tiny places only God sees
And from time to time He reminds us that we have yet to confess them
Even to Him
So we remain unforgiven

We lay our heads on bare chests and listen to our lies transmitted in morse code within the heartbeats of those men we love
And they are none the wiser
But we know
Our conscience is a constant reminder of sins we have committed
Our bodies are still laden with the devil's fingerprints
We can still feel his breath in our ears
His kisses on our lips
Yet we remain transfixed by his alluring smile
Becoming one with the part of ourselves we never identified with before
He sees right through us
Burns scarlet letters into our beings every time our paths cross
Piercing through the facade we put up for those who do not know any better
These good girls no one knows the truth about
And we don't really know those good girls anymore either
We have become too familiar with the darkest parts of who we are
Our consciences are always there as a reminder of what we'll never admit aloud
Those secret sins that we have buried deep within the threads of our inner workings
Skeletons within closets we dare not open
Or give credence to
Walking on eggshells hoping the bone collector doesn't decide to call us out on our farce
Afterall we are not completely at fault here
We are only doing karma's dirty work for her
And you gotta understand
It is impossible to stay clean when you have had such a satisfying sample

TABOO

Of what dirty feels like
If you look closely
You can see the scarlet undertones within our pigment now
And I can only speak for myself
I know that I am a good woman
But I must confess
Scarlet
has become my favorite color

Mermaid Confessions.

Ever since my father taught me to swim
By throwing me into the pool
I have never had to test the waters
I have grown accustomed to just jumping in
Whenever I feel like it
Sometimes I am pushed into the deep end
Without warning
Yet even then
I take my time coming up for air
I've learned I like being submerged in it
I love the way the water feels against my skin
Caressing every part of me
I have tried this whole walking-on-two-feet
Living-on-dry-land thing
And I end up disappointed every time
So instead I have chosen to swim
I have made my home in the ocean
Atlantis has beckoned
And for too long I have ignored its call
These days, I answer every one of them
I no longer desire this air I thought I once needed
These human elements no longer serve me
No longer beneficial to who I am
Or the path I am taking
I remember a time when I used to resist its pull

TABOO

But being submerged has become orgasmic
And who am I to deny myself such pleasure
It is in the water that I come alive
That I am able to be myself
And I am breathing just fine
Underneath it

Love Hard.

Our experiences teach us how to love
As children we are exposed to the right and wrong ways
So many wrong ways...
So many loves lost
And as a result of those experiences
I love hard
I love beyond reason
Beyond fault... to a fault
I love 'til heartbreak fits like a second skin
I love 'til emotional scars seep through and the facade of happiness is washed away
Like names etched in beach sand
With fingertips wrinkled from sea salt
I love like tomorrow doesn't exist
I love even though I know tomorrow doesn't exist
I love with all of me-
Every fiber of my being, every kinky coil atop my crown, every beat of my heart
I love until it hurts
Even though it hurts
And when it hurts-- I have learned to love through the pain
Like accidentally stepping on tiny shards of shattered glass
I've learned to tiptoe around the parts that truly hurt
To pretend they do not exist
To love without limits

TABOO

Limitless

I have learned the definition of love can be easily misconstrued
And the level I am on will never be experienced by you
Because my experiences have taught me
How to love
Hard
And without ceasing
Like initials carved in wet cement drying slowly and lasting over the years
I've learned to love like our love ain't going nowhere
Learned how to push aside logic and love despite opposition
Learned loving you is between you and me
And everyone on the outside is merely spectators to a sport we've grown to be so good at
And when we play
We play hard
Like calloused hands and men perpetrating like gangstas
We love like Cupid did a drive by
Stray bullet straight through our hearts
We love hopelessly like punctured arteries
And last breaths
And I promise to love you until my last breath
Inhaling your existence
Exhaling your promises of 'til death
'Cause with you I have learned love is hard
But not too hard that we cannot accomplish it
Hand in hand
Cheek to cheek
I vow to love you
Hard

'Cause that is all I know how to do
And you...
You make hard love
Look easy.

Dwelling Place.

Your arms remind me of home
A place I've read about in novels but never knew for myself
Until now
They reassure me that I am loved
That I am safe
Worth protecting
That I am valued
Your smile is a welcome mat at the front door
Letting me know it is okay
To walk inside
To remove my shoes
To lay down my burdens here
To take off my cape and mask
It reminds me that I can be fragile
That I do not need to save the world
That I can just exist inside of yours
If eyes are the windows to the soul
That would explain why I find peace in your gaze
I am sure my soul followed you here from whatever galaxy we began in
Because you just smell familiar
You smell like love
And magic
And coconut oil
A scent I can never get enough of
If you listen closely

You can hear the way our hearts beat in unison
A tune I cannot get out of my head
A reminder that love still exists
Even if I don't whisper its name
I know this is home
Because my heart is here
And it is whole
Once again

COCONUT OIL

"We will never forget
That sometimes finding freedom is more painful of an experience
Than living caged in black skin
Yet we will remain proud"
~excerpt *"After Nikki Giovanni"*

Lessons From My Dad... About God.

My dad taught us how to swim by throwing us into the swimming pool
Of whichever apartment complex we lived in at the time
With basic instructions and the most basic of human instincts to survive
We kicked our feet, moved our arms, and tried to make it to the surface on our own
Most times to no avail
And eventually we learned to just wait on him
At 4, 5, and 6-- my two sisters and I
like tadpoles became accustomed to being under water
And as if on cue, my daddy made it to each one of us just in time
Clearly, he wasn't much of the traditional kind
But my dad never came a moment too late
We
Never doubted he'd arrive or feared for our fate
Because we knew our dad would be there to save us
Just as he promised when he tossed us in
And though he wasn't the most dependable on dry land
When it came to that water
Our daddy was SuperMan
I mean, if SuperMan wasn't so much the flying type
I learned two obvious truths that remain true to this day
One: I can hold my breath for a very long time
And two: If I don't have goggles I'd drown out in the open sea because for the life of me I cannot swim above water and salt water burns the crap out of your eyes

TABOO

A full life in Miami has confirmed that
But those lessons in the pool taught me so much about life
And God
How our lives are similar to those waters
Sometimes like 3 ft,
shallow enough for us to stand on our own two
Or like 4 ft
with a little more depth but sustainable on our tippy toes
But sometimes life gets a little more difficult and requires more effort
like when in 5 ft
And then when God knows that we are ready
When God knows that it is time
We are thrown in 6 ft
With basic instructions and the most basic of human instincts to survive
At first we kick, and we cry, and we question, and we try
To do it on our own
Then with the wisdom of those little girls at age 4, 5, and 6
We learn to just wait
On our Heavenly Father
Because we know He will never leave nor forsake us
Because James 5 and 16 teaches us that the prayers of the righteous availeth much
And we know how to pray
And wait
With faith
We know our Father promised to save us if we only believe
And we always believed
Even while completely submerged and sitting on the bottom of life's swimming pool

Weighed down by struggles and tribulations
By experiences we never imagined would be our own
And while under water we make sure to keep our mouths shut
Because we know it is impossible to breathe underwater
While speaking doubt into the atmosphere
We know we can get a little more oxygen into our lungs and last a little while longer
If we remain calm and swallow when it seems we are running out of breath
And so we swallow
Our fears
We abandon the parts of ourselves that want to convince us if we try a little harder
We can get to the surface without Him
And we embrace the lessons of our daddy
His actions which inadvertently taught us to believe in God's word
And most importantly to wait on the Lord
To show up
With outstretched arms
And a reassuring smile
To save us from this pool just like our dad always did
These days
Our daddy can't do much saving for his little girls turned women
But without trying
His swim lessons have taught us
About a Father who can and always will
Save us
Right on time

Dejavu.

She asked
"Mommy, why does this keep happening?"
And I was reminded of 2013 when the verdict in Trayvon Martin's murder was delivered
Of 2014 with the murder of Eric Garner.
And Michael Brown.
And Tamir Rice.
Of 2015 with Freddie Gray.
And Walter Scott.
And Samuel Dubose.
Of 2016 with the murder of Alton Sterling.
And Terrence Crutcher.

Not guilty.

But this time
Although there was no murder
I had no explanation
I could not find the words to explain why this unarmed person of color was shot
By police
As he sat in his vehicle
Alarm blaring
Simply trying to get it to stop malfunctioning

This pig
Shot him twice

Once in the back
Once in the stomach
For good measure

Over a fucking alarm.

Lyndo Jones
Survived

And I said a silent prayer of 'thanks' that he was alive to share his story
To control his narrative
Which would have undoubtedly been written another way had he
succumbed to his injuries
Thankful that his voice would be heard
That he wouldn't need to become somebody's hashtag
Thankful that there would be no need for a hashtag
this time

But she could only wonder about why it happened in the first place
Her eleven year old innocence could not decipher the underlying message of
hate transcribed within the lines of this newscast
She didn't understand
And that morning I did not have the nerve to break it to her

But I left that car a little more broken than usual

TABOO

Her question pierced the part of my soul I thought had frozen over
I ran to a friend's classroom and cried
Grasping for sanity before the bell would ring and my students would rush in
She hugged me, providing a brief moment of comfort
I grabbed the last kleenex and wiped away the evidence of my brokenness

At least he is alive

At least he is alive

At least.

No. You Cannot Touch My Hair.

I never wanted to be white
With blonde hair and blue eyes
Never wanted to be a brunette
Or a redhead
I never desired white baby dolls that looked nothing like me for my pretend family with my pretend husband and our pretend children
I didn't grow up with a curiosity to see how the other side lives
Never wanted to touch some white child's hair because it was so obviously different from my own
Yet so many see my kinky coils and the intrigue burns through their spirit like crosses on Baptist church lawns
And they just cannot resist the question begging to be freed from their lips
To date I have been asked one thousand two hundred ninety five times
And yes, that is a rough estimate
But people are not shy about treating my kind like animals at a petting zoo
I guess our fur is just too fascinating to not reach out and pet our heads
To not cure that curiosity and answer the age old question of whether or not it feels like the cotton we used to pick for massa'
Or some rough Brillo pads used to scrub dishes clean
Or the reality they never expect
That it just feels like what it is
Just human hair
And not just any old hair

TABOO

This hair is my crown
Given to me by God himself
And when is the last time someone asked Queen Elizabeth to touch her crown
How dare you feel so comfortable to insult a black queen
Do you walk into a museum and ask to touch the artifacts located there
Do you walk into a gallery and ask to touch the paintings hanging there
Do I require red rope and signs hanging saying Do Not Touch in order for you to comprehend what common sense should advise without my saying No. You cannot touch my hair.
Yes. I am dead serious.
Yes. I am also offended.
And yes. I feel sorry for you for even wanting to
Because I am guessing your parents didn't love you enough to teach you the story of how curiosity killed the cat
And since black don't crack we will gladly share our age if asked
But one thing you should never do
Is ask to touch a black woman's hair
Or her ass while we're on the subject of things you better keep your hands off of
But this hair is not to be messed with
Do not stare at me like you have seen the antichrist in the flesh
Do not make some stupid joke about some other black person's hair you saw recently just like mine
Or would you mind if I compared you to every female of your race with a pixie cut, or a bob, or bleached bangs with dark roots
This is not some African movement
For black pride Or black panthers
This is just who I am

An African
In America
With great hair
U mad
Or nah?

TABOO

After Nikki Giovanni.

"...for those whose freedom was found at the end of a rope."

You had the nerve to be born black
With skin tainted by pigment with too much melanin to be anything but condemned
We have never been more than black skin to them
To a people still ignorant enough to hate us for that very reason
Yet paint themselves in black face
Emulating our sun-kissed essence for their entertainment
Our men remain targeted for being born kings
Our women are oversexualized beings
Our children are undervalued
And we have grown comfortable living with the weight of the world on our shoulders
Boots of our enemies pressed against our necks daring them to break
But we are resilient people
We are brilliant people
Treading through the muddy waters of life seeking freedom
Some are ignorant enough to believe we have attained after all these years
But we know better
We've been shown better
Those ropes and lynchings of our innocent are now replaced by Klansmen in uniform
They shoot first and never ask questions
Or provide answers

For how unarmed men, boys, women, and girls
Can be shot multiple times
Down like dogs
Their families told to suck it up and move on
This is for those whose freedom was found at the end of a rope
For those whose freedom was found at the end of the barrel of a smoking gun
For those who have the audacity to be black
And proud
To be black
And unashamed
To be black
And live as if it doesn't matter that they are black
Those who aren't seeking freedom at all but stumble upon it
On the day before their weddings
On the train while heading home with friends
Down the street from their father's house by neighborhood watchmen with god complexes
In suburban neighborhoods innocently seeking help after car crashes
In their high school gymnasiums rolled up in gym mats
In front of their homes while reaching for their wallets to identify themselves
This is for the freedom they would never experience on this side of the horizon
As black men and black women
With targets on their backs from the day they were born
Who are murdered with so much potential buried within their bones
With dreams they didn't know they were never gonna see come into fruition

TABOO

Because the stars didn't align the way we all hoped
And so with so much hope
We fight and we march
We protest and we pray
And we cry
For those we have lost
And we cry
For those we will lose
And we cry
For our little boys and girls who we fear will stumble upon the same so-called freedom
Eerily found at the end of the rope
Or a smoking gun
In the hands of some coward
With preconceived notions about this black skin
This
Is in your memory
In memory of all of our innocent we will never be able to name
one by one
And in honor of your memory
We will never forget
That sometimes finding freedom is more painful of an experience
Than living caged in black skin
Yet we will remain proud
And brave
And we will live
Just as you died
Unashamed
And

Unafraid
To be
Beautiful
So beautiful
And
Black

Magic.

The weight of it all
Is often too heavy a burden
To carry
In this skin that I love
In this body
They wish wouldn't exist
In these bones that are home to pure magic
That house the very existence of Alpha and Omega in them
The weight of the world on these shoulders
But head still raised
As I balance this crown
Blooming from my scalp
Like daisies
Flourishing in African soil
How beautiful
From the distance
You almost cannot smell the stench of rotting flesh
hidden beneath the aroma of black excellence in the air
And that is magic
It is a living thing
Isn't it
Such a heavy thing
To be hated
Despite your love of self
To be maimed

And murdered
Though we fight
Daily
To be remembered as more than just hashtags
Our very breath is an act of resistance
And so we can't wait any longer
for change to come
We must act now

So rise up
Square up
Level up
Stand up
It is time
To take back what is ours
To show the world what this magic is all about

The End

~ About The Poet ~

Born February 9, 1986, Arnetta "TABOO" Bullard is a proud native of Miami, Fl. Raised by her paternal grandparents, Lula and Lawrence Roberts, in the Brown Sub community, she learned early on about trials, tribulations, and the importance of a relationship with God.

Her early childhood was far from storybook perfect and could only be described as tumultuous and traumatizing. With a drug-addicted mother and abusive father, Arnetta Gordon learned about rejection, heartbreak, and distrust before other children her age. She began writing to God within personal journals to express her innermost thoughts and these journals became the foundation for her love of writing and creative expression.

TABOO is a poet, spoken-word artist, writer, educator, and motivational speaker. She can now add PUBLISHED AUTHOR to her list of credentials. Faced with tragedy when she was 12-years-old, she stumbled upon her gift while writing several poems in memory of a childhood friend, Demetric Tywan Malloy, who was killed by gun violence at the age of 16. During the time of his death, she became acutely aware of her God-given gift of poetry, prose, and all things literary.

TABOO graduated high school with honors and went on to earn her Bachelor's degree in Secondary Education with a concentration in English in 2013. She is currently an English teacher and English Department Chairperson at a charter school in Miami, FL.

TABOO

Naturally gifted, TABOO is one of Miami's hidden poetic gems. Although she has performed at various locations around the Miami and Ft Lauderdale area, the full potential of her abilities are yet to be seen. Aside from performances at well-known poetic venues, TABOO has spoken at various charity and women empowerment events.

She first hit the stage under the watchful eye of DefJam poet, Will "DaRealOne" Bell, inside of his venue- The Literary Café. His willingness to provide a platform to help shape her gift left an undeniable impression upon her and inspired her to work meticulously on getting better and better. He saw something within her during a time when she doubted her ability to compare to the plethora of talented poets in the Miami area and around the world. Naturally, a friendship developed and to this day the wisdom he imparted has become the soundtrack to her endeavors. His death in 2011 forever changed the poetry community nationwide and had a personal effect on her life. Though initially frozen by his death, in his honor- she vows to continue pursuing her passion and perfecting her gifts.

She writes to motivate, inform, persuade, and entertain. She speaks as a beacon of power motivating those under the sound of her voice. Never playing into the stereotypical role of a woman, she speaks without censor- blunt truths of her reality and the world around her.

Blunt. Honest. Open. Passionate. Inspiring. She is the truth--- and that truth is TABOO.

Made in the USA
Columbia, SC
03 March 2023